DRAWING ANIMALS

DRAWING ANIMALS

Learn How to Draw Everything from Dogs, Sharks, and Dinosaurs to Cats, Llamas, and More!

Lise Herzog

BLOOM BOOKS
FOR YOUNG READERS

First published in 2020 as *Dessiner les animaux - 50 modèles pour débuter* in Paris, France, by Editions Mango.

Published by:
Bloom Books for Young Readers,
an imprint of Ulysses Press
PO Box 3440
Berkeley, CA 94703
www.ulyssespress.com

ISBN: 978-1-64604-157-2

10 9 8 7 6 5 4 3 2 1

Acquisitions editor: Keith Riegert
Managing editor: Claire Chun
Editors: Kate St.Clair, Renee Rutledge
Front cover design: Flor Figueroa
Interior design and layout: what!design @ whatweb.com

TABLE OF CONTENTS

GETTING STARTED

Drawing Animals is all about positioning shapes into two dimensions so that they are wild, fluid, and moving, with the ability to jump off the page. Don't freeze your animals on paper with clean contours and highly detailed features. Instead, bring your animals to life with the techniques I will teach you in this book. Your work will stay in motion with the bare minimum of necessary detail—letting the imagination breathe life into the animal.

You can group animals together by their common features. In these "families," many of the animals' general forms will be similar, but the details will change. Once you know how to draw an animal, it will be easy to draw others from the same group. This book offers basic sketches of animal families, such as marine mammals, rodents, and cats, and it will be up to you to complete the details specific to other animals that are not featured here.

Some animals have proportions and shapes that seem too difficult to faithfully reproduce. Noticing details is essential. When re-creating these animals, try variations such as stretching the legs, shortening the muzzle, or lengthening the ears. Adding unique details and presenting an overall impression are what count, much more than replicating the proportions exactly.

Before you start, study your animal subject and try to imagine that it's transparent. Visualize the different layers it is made of and how it compares to other animals. Mapping the various sizes of the animal's features, limbs, and joints will help you flesh out its full shape.

Start by drawing a base made of simple shapes before adding body contours and details. For this step, it is best to use a graphite pencil, which allows you to start your drawing lightly enough that it can be easily erased.

When you're done with your initial sketch, add detail using any drawing tool you prefer. Pencils, as used in the shark drawing below, accommodate light or dark shading, depending on how much pressure you apply to the tip. Pens and markers allow for a consistent intensity of black and are great for curved lines. Ballpoint pens draw both soft, light lines and dark lines.

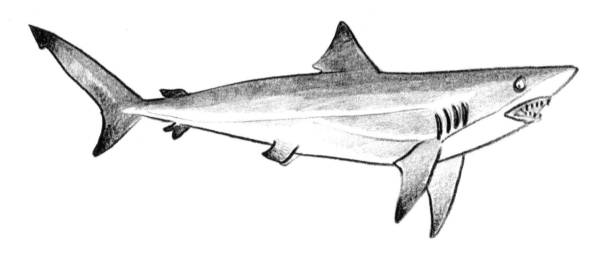

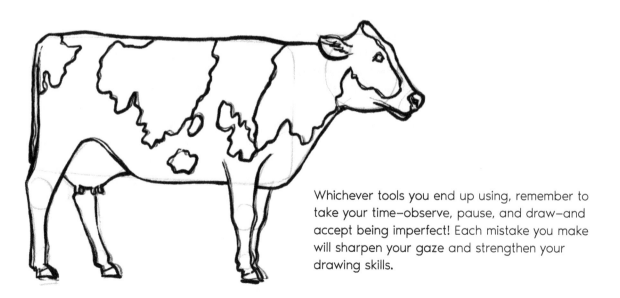

Whichever tools you end up using, remember to take your time—observe, pause, and draw—and accept being imperfect! Each mistake you make will sharpen your gaze and strengthen your drawing skills.

MARINE ANIMALS

For most marine animals, it's best to start the body by drawing a curve similar to an inverted comma shape. Each species will have unique features that you can add later; but generally, the head should be placed on the thickest side of the body (the decimal point of the comma). It's important to keep the body looking flexible and sinuous.

After drawing the dolphin's body, add more features like the dorsal fin, the triangle-shaped tail, and—one of the more unique characteristics for dolphins—the snout.

Draw the two small fins near the head like small wings, with one behind the other to make your drawing look more three-dimensional. Then re-sketch the contours and add a few more line details to give your dolphin a wet, sleek look—like it's swimming in the ocean.

Porpoises have compact heads and small, triangular snouts, so make sure to highlight those features. Then add additional detail to make your drawing really stand out.

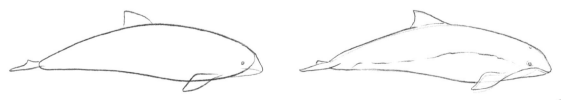

Whales, on the other hand, have stretched-out snouts, and their fins are farther down the sides of the body than a dolphin's fins. Recognizing and applying these different proportion details is guaranteed to make your drawing look amazing and accurate!

Sharks are easy to identify because of their prominent snouts, rows of sharp teeth, and, of course, the pointed dorsal fin.

Some fish can have very unusual features, like the hammerhead shark, whose head is perpendicular to the line of its body!

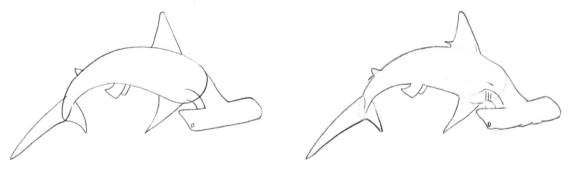

FINISH YOUR DRAWING
WITH A BLACK PENCIL

With a black pencil, you can draw lines that are dark and rich, or soft and powdery if you don't press too hard. However, be careful because lines made with this pencil don't blend well.

First, redraw the marine animal with the black pencil. Then erase the original gray pencil lines as much as possible.

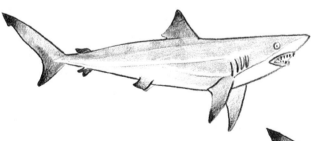

To add "color" to the body, press lightly on the tip of your pencil and shade certain areas. This will create a soft-looking surface.

Gradually darken parts of your drawing to bring out the shape of the body and to add small details to the fins. When drawing a shark, make sure to keep the stomach clear.

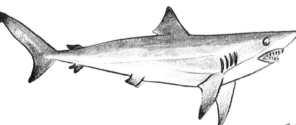

SHARK PRACTICE PAGES

Try your hand at finishing the original sketch.

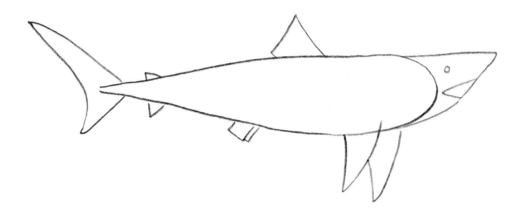

Draw your own shark below.

RODENTS AND WEASELS

Most small rodents have a large lower body and much smaller upper body. Rodents are very agile, with hind legs that are noticeably bigger than their front legs. They can easily curl into a ball, sit up, or stretch out their entire body to run and jump. These unique details make rodents different from other animals.

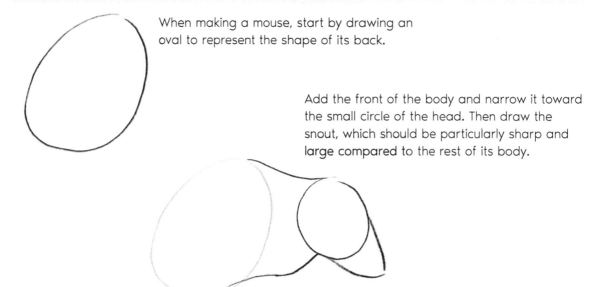

When making a mouse, start by drawing an oval to represent the shape of its back.

Add the front of the body and narrow it toward the small circle of the head. Then draw the snout, which should be particularly sharp and large compared to the rest of its body.

Draw the ears relatively large, and add a tail that's long and tapered at the end.

Unlike the mouse, the groundhog has a rounder head, small ears, and a bushy tail.

Make everything in the ferret's body more stretched out.

Hamsters like to sit up on their hind legs when something catches their attention.

If you view a hamster from the front, its body looks like many round shapes stacked on top of each other.

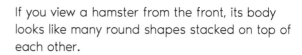

FINISH YOUR DRAWING WITH A FELT-TIP MARKER

With a medium-thick felt-tip marker, you can create nuanced lines that are either thick or thin, depending on how hard you press. A tool like this makes it easy to highlight small details and darken certain areas.

Redraw the outer edges of your rodent and add small zigzag patterns to bring out the texture of its coat.

After erasing some of your original pencil lines, add a few more details.

Cover the body with fine lines, making sure to leave some white areas to keep the fur light. The groundhog here has a relatively thick coat.

The more you darken certain parts, the more you bring out the shape and depth of the groundhog's body. Just don't go overboard with the shading, or you might weigh down your drawing!

GROUNDHOG PRACTICE PAGES

Try your hand at finishing the original sketch.

Draw your own groundhog in the space below.

BEARS AND KOALAS

The creatures in this favorite "stuffed animal" family often appear large and bulky, mainly because of their thick fur. Most bears have small, round heads and stand on short legs. Sometimes you'll even see bears sit up by resting their big bodies on their slighter hind legs!

You can recognize a bear by its small head and broad shoulders, so it's easiest to start by drawing these features. Now connect these body parts with long, flexible curves.

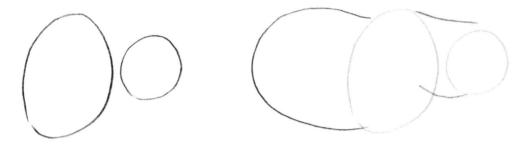

You can draw a bear's feet to look a little bit like slippers. Then give it a muzzle that's long and flat at the end, and add some small, round ears.

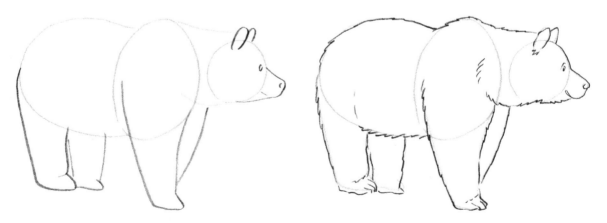

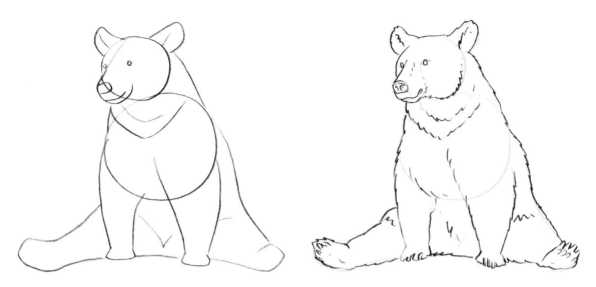

When a bear is sitting, draw it to look like its body mass has piled up. Use guidelines to sketch a muzzle from the front—you want it to point slightly downward.

The panda is slightly rounder and more upright than other bears. Pandas also have bigger heads and a very recognizable black and white coat.

Bears can also possess certain postures that might help you recognize the animal. Pandas, for example, like to cross an arm over their chest.

The koala is stockier than the rest, with long front paws, fluffy, wide ears, and a recognizably round head.

FINISH YOUR DRAWING WITH A GRAY PENCIL

For these sketches, you'll want to use graphite pencils with intensities that vary from 4B (medium dark) to 6B (dark) on the graphite grading scale. These pencils allow you to create very dark, thick lines as well as light gray surfaces, depending on how hard you press. Try blending the drawing by rubbing certain lines with a kneaded eraser, a finger, or a cardboard blending stump.

Redraw the outline of the body and give your bear or koala a thick, ruffled coat.

Try to erase the original body outline as much as possible. Sketch small, light lines on the body and rub to blend them together, giving the fur a soft look.

Finish the fur coat by leaving a few unshaded, white areas.

If you enhance the shading on one side of the body, your bear or koala will look more rounded and realistic.

Darken a few details and add some more small lines to make the coat bushier.

KOALA PRACTICE PAGES

Try your hand at finishing the original sketch.

Draw your own koala in the space below.

CATS

Cats are very flexible, with bodies that can tighten into in a ball or quickly stretch out. This one here has a body that looks like a bag with a small, circular head. The larger the cat, the more its body parts will gain power and thickness. Those details, and the unique patterns of the coat, are what make cats so recognizable.

This cat has a small, round head with a long body extending behind it.

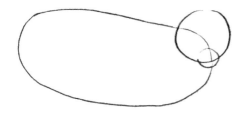

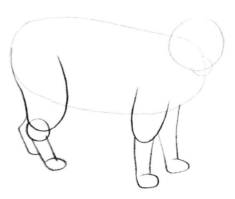

Unlike human legs, a cat's hind legs have distinct "knees" (which are actually ankles) that bend slightly backward.

After the long tail and triangle-shaped ears have been drawn, it's obvious that this animal is a cat.

Different perspectives will change the shape of the body. Sometimes the lower back may appear smaller, and the head may need to be drawn with straight lines instead of a circle.

Every part of the cat will be more stretched when it is jumping. The rear thigh becomes much more visible in a jump position, so clearly define it by drawing a circle.

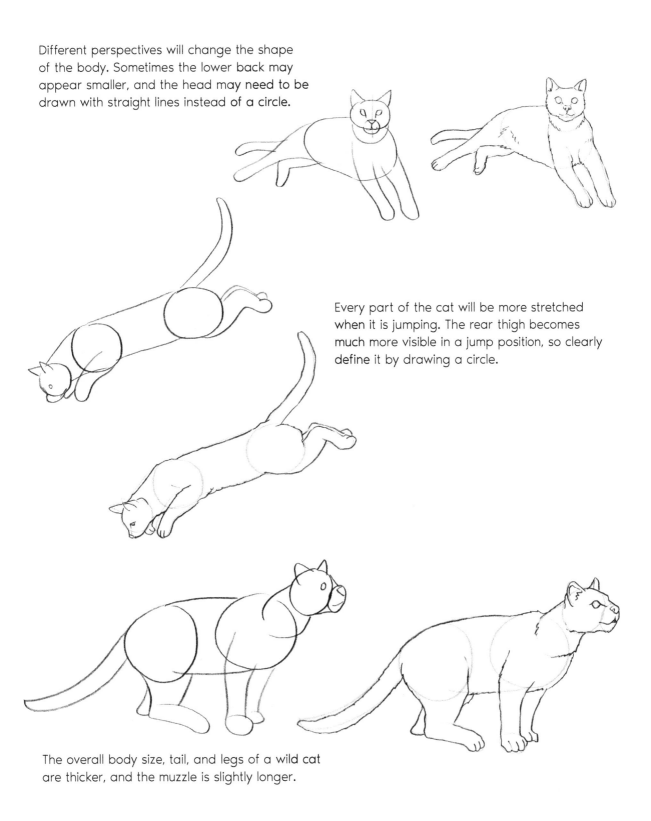

The overall body size, tail, and legs of a wild cat are thicker, and the muzzle is slightly longer.

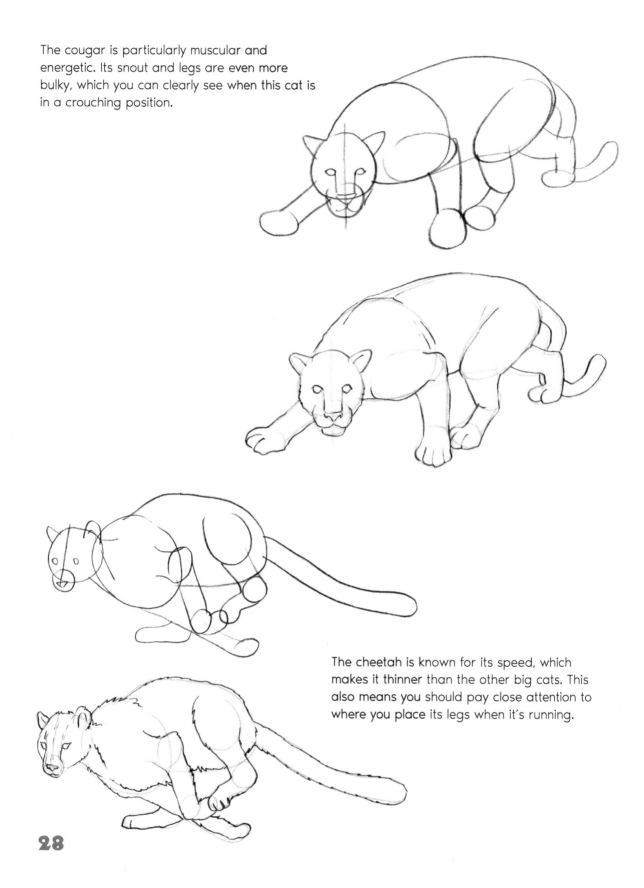

The cougar is particularly muscular and energetic. Its snout and legs are even more bulky, which you can clearly see when this cat is in a crouching position.

The cheetah is known for its speed, which makes it thinner than the other big cats. This also means you should pay close attention to where you place its legs when it's running.

28

FINISH YOUR DRAWING WITH A GRAPHITE PENCIL

Graphite brings a softness to the drawing that other pencils do not. Without pressing too hard, it's easy to create gray, blended areas. If you want darker lines, be sure to press harder.

Finish your drawing by sketching with a hard black (HB) graphite pencil after you erase some of the original guidelines near the center of the body.

Next, draw tight, small lines without pressing too hard. Make sure to leave some white patches for the cats that have lighter colored coats.

Adding a second layer of fine lines on part of the coat will make it darker there.

Pressing harder can bring out more details.

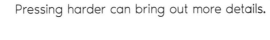

Add some final patterns to the coat.

29

HOUSE CAT PRACTICE PAGES

Try your hand at finishing the original sketch.

Draw your own cat in the space below.

SMALL DOGS

A dog's body shape is usually the opposite of a cat's. Some distinct characteristics of dogs include shoulders that are wider than their lower backs, a more prominent neck, and legs that are fairly thin and short.

When a dog has short hair, like the Jack Russell, you can easily see the details of its various body parts. To make a dog that's slightly muscular, use lines and circles to draw the separate areas of the body.

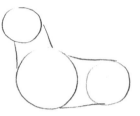

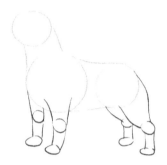

Draw an extended muzzle, floppy ears, and a pointed tail.

As you draw the contours of the body, refine all the body details you drew earlier.

Some dogs are unique and have many folds of skin on their body.

If the dog has a long fur coat, it is easier to concentrate on drawing general shapes of the body rather than specific proportions.

Sometimes, the position of the dog or the length of their fur hides their paws or other body parts.

FINISH YOUR DRAWING WITH A FELT-TIP PEN AND PENCIL

You can use very different tools, like a felt-tip pen and a pencil, on the same drawing. The pen produces thick black lines, and the pencil is great for creating fine hatching or shading.

A thicker tool is better for the contours. Felt-tip markers help cover up those initial guidelines.

With the pencil, gradually add small hatches to create shadows.

By pressing harder on the pencil, you can darken areas and create different patterns on the fur coat.

Pencil lines are perfect for drawing long hairs, if your dog has a shaggy fur coat.

34

JACK RUSSELL PRACTICE PAGES

Try your hand at finishing the original Jack Russell sketch.

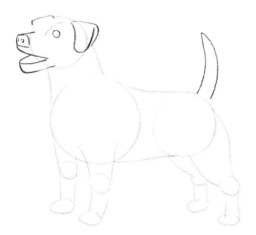

Draw your own Jack Russell in the space below.

YORKSHIRE TERRIER PRACTICE PAGES

Try your hand at finishing the original Yorkshire Terrier sketch.

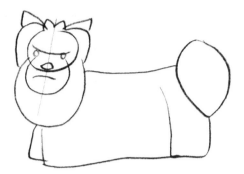

Draw your own Yorkshire Terrier in the space below.

HOOFED ANIMALS

Deer belong to a family of medium-sized animals that have long, thin legs and sharp hooves. Their heads are small and round, their necks somewhat long, and their snouts slightly elongated.

When drawing a larger animal, it's best to start with the head, which will help guide the posture and the size of the other body parts. Draw a long, graceful neck extending from the head. Then add a guideline for the snout.

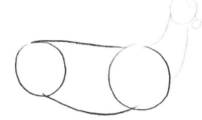

The back of a deer's body is slightly thinner than the front. The body as a whole should appear much larger than the head.

Draw some thin legs with defined joints so that the rest of the body seems heavy compared to the legs.

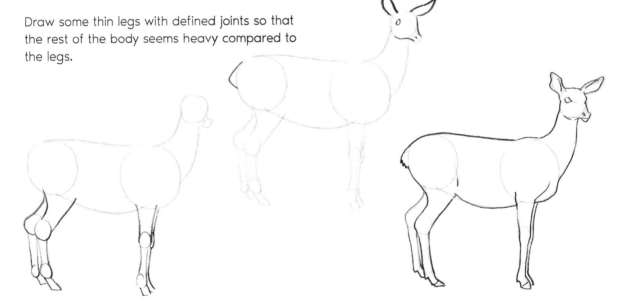

A doe has large. leaf-shaped ears that point upward.

Compared to a deer, the goat has a larger
body near the back, slightly shorter legs, and a
goatee and horns!

The sheep's fluffy coat often hides the different
shapes of the body, so it's best to focus on
drawing the volume of its coat.

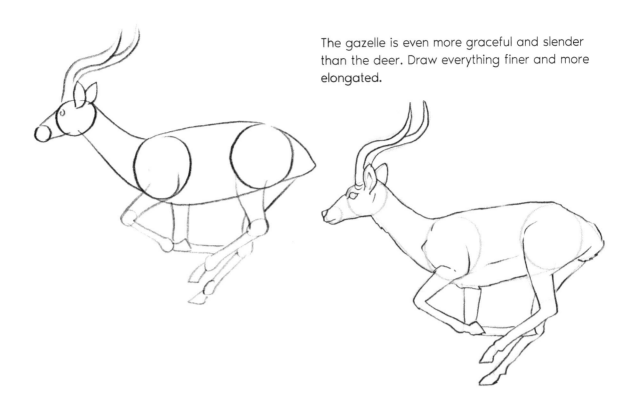

The gazelle is even more graceful and slender than the deer. Draw everything finer and more elongated.

On the other hand, the ibex is stockier and more muscular.

FINISH YOUR DRAWING WITH A BLACK PENCIL

There is a wide variety of drawing pencils, apart from graphite pencils, that feature different intensities and colors. Some, like the black pencil, are drier than other colored pencils and, therefore, produce a finer line.

Once the animal's outline is drawn, erase as much of the guidelines as possible and add some patterns to the body.

With fine hatching, shade in gray areas, which will create more depth.

As you gradually darken more areas of the coat by adding new hatch layers, make sure to keep a few lighter parts, too.

Finish by adding more details on the hooves, eyes, and ears, as well as on the upper side of the coat.

DEER PRACTICE PAGES

Try your hand at finishing the original sketch.

Draw your own deer in the space below.

EQUINE FAMILY

In the equine family, not all animals are as tall and slender as the horse, but most of these animals have the same proportions: a large body and delicate, thin legs.

The donkey has a fairly large head compared to the rest of its body, and its neck is shorter than a horse's neck.

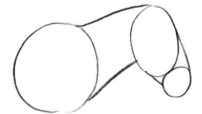

While the front and back of the body are the same size, the donkey's stomach is very round.

Make the legs as delicate as you can, with distinct joints marked by small circles.

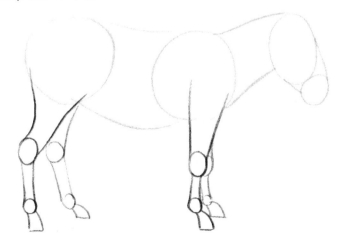

Donkeys have large, pointy ears and a brush-like tail.

Add some final details that will make the donkey recognizable.

Zebras really stand out because of their mane and the black tip of their snout. And, of course, the pattern of their coat!

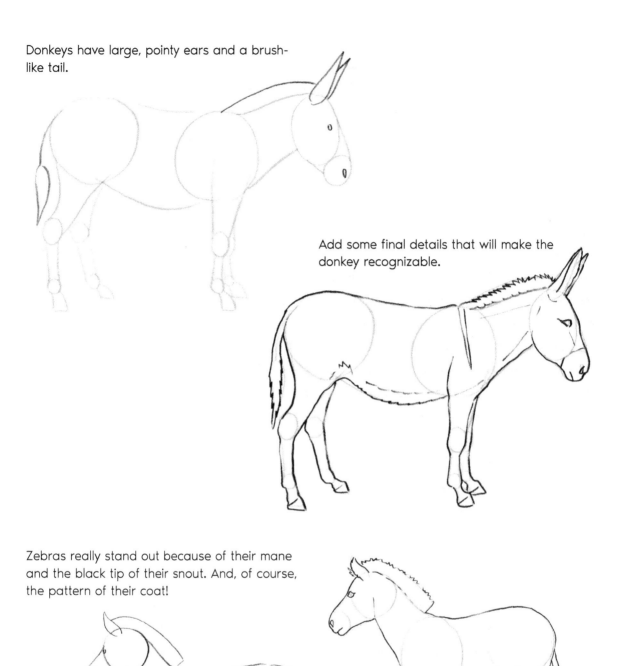

As with any equine, when you draw a zebra running, pay close attention to how the legs are oriented. Make sure they don't just go forward or backward.

When you draw an animal from this perspective, the body parts that are farther away look smaller than those in the foreground.

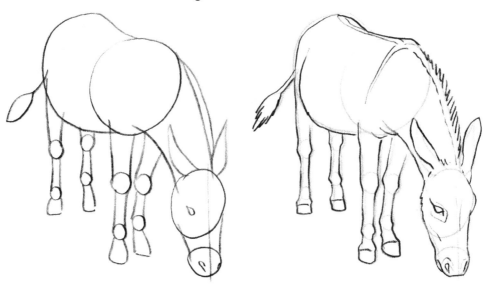

FINISH YOUR DRAWING WITH A CHARCOAL PENCIL

Charcoal pencils are dark and powdery. If you carve it into a fine point, you can draw very thin lines with it. You can then blur these lines by rubbing them with your finger or a cardboard blending stump. Charcoal generates a lot of extra powder, so you might have to blow on it to remove it from your drawing.

Start by outlining your animal.

Then carefully erase as much of the guidelines as possible.

Next, start to add small shadows along the outline of the body.

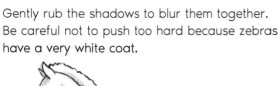

Gently rub the shadows to blur them together. Be careful not to push too hard because zebras have a very white coat.

Finally, add the most unique characteristic. For a zebra, that would be its stripes.

ZEBRA PRACTICE PAGES

Try your hand at finishing the original sketch.

Draw your own zebra in the space below.

LLAMAS AND OTHER CAMELIDS

The llama is part of an animal family that features large bodies perched on long, thin legs—characteristics that make them easily identifiable. These animals also have a small head set on a tall, curved neck and a snout that is thin with a flat, broad tip.

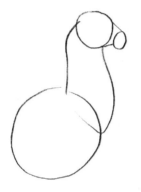

It's easiest to start by drawing the llama's head. Then decide how curved you want the neck to be.

Because llamas have a thick fur coat, add a lot of volume to the back and stomach.

Draw the legs thin and partly cover along the top with fur.

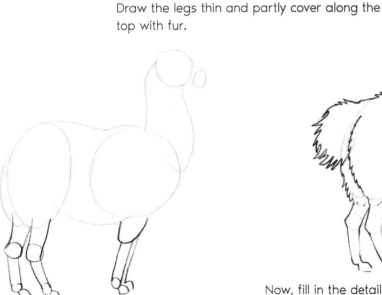

Now, fill in the details: a bushy tail, large ears, and a clearly defined snout.

The camel is larger and longer than the llama, but its fur coat isn't as thick, making the body shapes more visible. The camel also has two humps on its back, and the tip of its snout is thicker.

Like the camel, the dromedary (aka the Arabian camel) stands on legs that seem disproportionate to the large volume of its body. However, this camel has only one hump. Looking at it from the front, you can also clearly see its thicker muzzle.

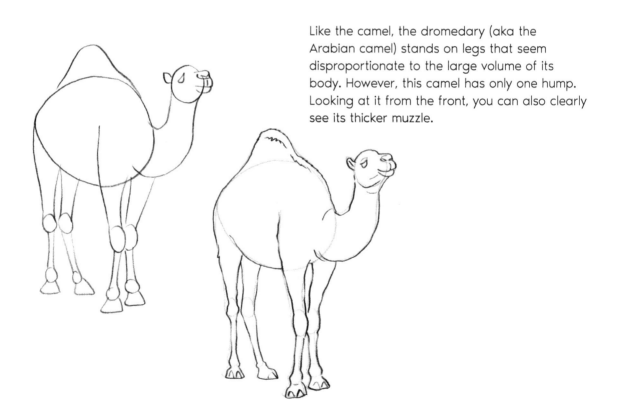

FINISH YOUR DRAWING
WITH A FINE PENCIL

The fine pencil is not made to fill in large, dark areas. Instead, this pencil is perfect for creating dry, sharp lines—use it to draw delicate details.

When redrawing the contours of this sketch, add some long, fine lines going in different directions to create a long fur coat.

Add a layer of hatching to create shadows and add some more dimension.

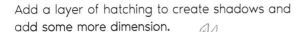

Intensify the shadows by adding another layer of hatching on top of the first.

Make the lighter parts of the coat stand out so the fur looks even more bushy.

Finish your drawing by darkening more of the details and shadows.

LLAMA PRACTICE PAGES

Try your hand at finishing the original sketch.

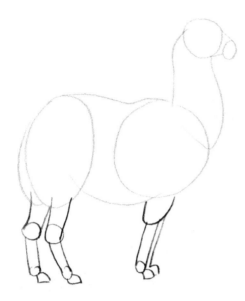

Draw your own llama in the space below.

BOVINES

Some animals, like cows, have massive bodies and short legs. Their bodies are quite angular and can look like a rectangle, depending on the angle. They also have large heads with relatively thick snouts.

To draw a cow, start by drawing a large rectangle.

Choose an upper corner, and draw the neck and head.

When drawing the legs, remember they are quite thin and shorter than donkey or horse legs.

Add some finishing touches to the head and, if your cow has any, draw some spots on the body.

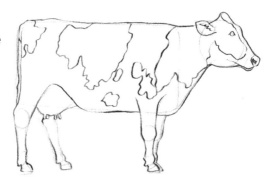

The bull is visibly more muscular than the cow, so its body parts are usually rounder.

A bison has much more detail at the front of its body than the back. It also has a flattened head and a neck that appears shorter because it's covered with fur.

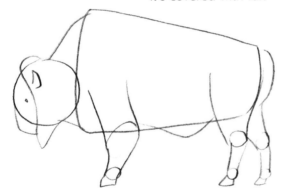 

The water buffalo has a big snout and large horns.

FINISH YOUR DRAWING WITH THICK, CHISEL-TIP FELT MARKERS

This tool allows you to create dark, thick lines and thinner, more delicate lines—if you don't press too hard. You can also experiment with line thickness by orienting the tip in different ways.

Start by redrawing the animal, pressing lightly with the thin part of the chisel-tip felt pen.

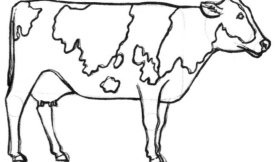

Add a few more details, and then erase as much of the original pencil lines as possible.

Using fine, light hatching, use shading to give your bovine more dimension.

Finally, fill in the details, as done with this cow's black spots.

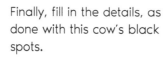

COW PRACTICE PAGES

Try your hand at finishing the original sketch.

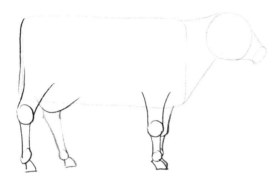

Draw your own cow in the space below.

SMALL BIRDS

Most small- and medium-sized birds have a body in the shape of a leaning water drop. The widest part of the water drop is near the neck and the pointed end is where the tail starts. It's the details surrounding this water drop that will make each bird unique.

To begin drawing a pigeon, start with a long, leaning water drop.

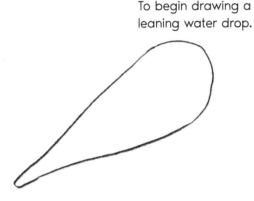

Next, add the neck and a round head, and decide what size you want the beak to be.

Remember to keep the legs short and the beak very pointed.

Now, outline some feather patterns.

Magpies have a rounder body.

Seagulls are perched slightly higher on their legs, and their bodies are often perpendicular to them.

Blackbirds appear very composed and round,
with a mobile tail.

When a dove is in flight, its spread wings
are shaped like triangles and show off each
feather. The tail is also fanned out.

A flying seagull has much larger wings, and its
beak is long and thick.

FINISH YOUR DRAWING WITH DIFFERENT PENCILS

To create different shades of gray and black, use multiple pencils on the same drawing rather than pressing harder or softer on a single tool.

It's best to use the darkest and thickest pencil you have to outline the drawing.

After erasing as much of the original construction lines as possible, darken parts of the bird's plumage.

Add some dark touches to the wing feathers without covering them entirely, so that the wings stay visible.

Darken a few of the shaded areas even more.

With a lighter pencil, add small touches of shading on the stomach and wings.

BIRD PRACTICE PAGES

Try your hand at finishing the original sketch.

Draw your own bird in the space below.

BIG BIRDS

In the bird family, some birds have slender, elongated legs, outstretched necks, and longer beaks.

Similar to the bodies of small birds, start your heron sketch with a leaning water drop shape that points downward.

Add a long S-shaped neck and a small oval for the head.

Draw the legs long and thin, with round and distinct joints.

Finish adding the small details, like the lean and lengthy bill.

Add a few tufts of feathers as you outline the contours of the body.

The flamingo has large, round wings and a big, hooked beak.

Storks often have shorter necks. When in flight, the tips of their wings are separated by large feathers.

In flight, an egret's spread wings are sharp. A long, thin feather at the back of its head also makes it unique.

FINISH YOUR DRAWING WITH AN INK PEN

Ink pens are a smart choice because there's no need to constantly dip the pen in ink, making it easy to avoid stains. However, depending on the type of pen you use, it might be hard to tell the difference between solid, thick lines and hairlines.

Start by redrawing the contours and give your bird a few feather details.

After erasing the original construction lines, use hatching to create some shadows. Be careful to leave a few light areas to maintain the bird's dimensions.

Adding feathers will give more volume to the wings.

You can continue to add more line details, but make sure not to overdo it.

FLAMINGO PRACTICE PAGES

Try your hand at finishing the original sketch.

Draw your own flamingo in the space below.

REPTILES

The majority of reptiles have extended bodies with short legs, if they have any legs at all. Their bodies are often covered in rough skin and feature various patterns ranging from very simple to highly complicated.

To draw a crocodile, it is best to start with the shape and orientation of its body. Use a curved line to indicate the tail.

At the open end of the body, add a circle for the head and finish the other end with a pointed tail.

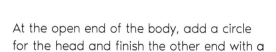

A crocodile's jaw hangs on its head. Depending on how you orient your drawing, the jaw can be somewhat complicated to draw, especially if it's open. After you sketch out the jaw, add a few lines going down the tail to mark out future skin patterns.

Because the legs are thick and short, there is no need to depict joints. Draw large claws at the ends of the feet.

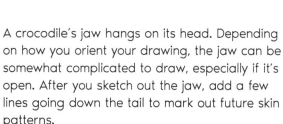

Outline the shape of the body so you can start drawing the scales. Then add some sharp teeth.

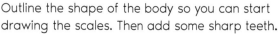

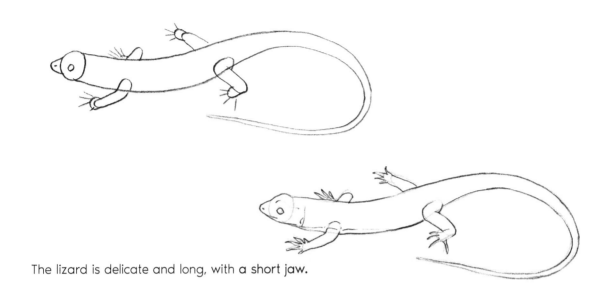

The lizard is delicate and long, with a short jaw.

The chameleon has a few recognizable details: large eyes, curled tail, and long legs that look like they end in fingers.

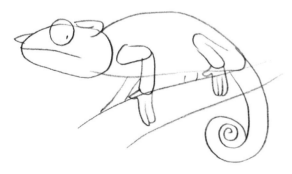

FINISH YOUR DRAWING WITH INK

The pen is an edged tool that can create both solid lines and hairlines—but if you press too hard, the ink may leak.

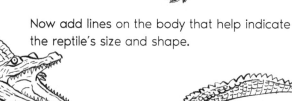

Start by redrawing the reptile with somewhat wiggly lines, depending on how you want to portray it. Really shaky lines can mean your reptile is rough and dangerous, while smoother lines make it appear sleek and calm. Then erase the original pencil lines.

Now add lines on the body that help indicate the reptile's size and shape.

Between these lines, draw smaller lines or other shapes to create rough skin patterns.

Using fine hatching, create shadows and dimension. Don't forget to fill in the inside of the mouth to provide even more depth.

Finally, accentuate the shadows in a few areas.

CROCODILE PRACTICE PAGES

Try your hand at finishing the original sketch.

Draw your own crocodile in the space below.

DINOSAURS

Since a wide variety of dinosaurs exist, it's impossible to classify them into families. Dinosaurs come in even the most improbable forms, sizes, and shapes.

The easiest way to start drawing a diplodocus is by sketching a huge, long neck that ends with a very small, round head. The size of the body will look ridiculously small compared to its neck.

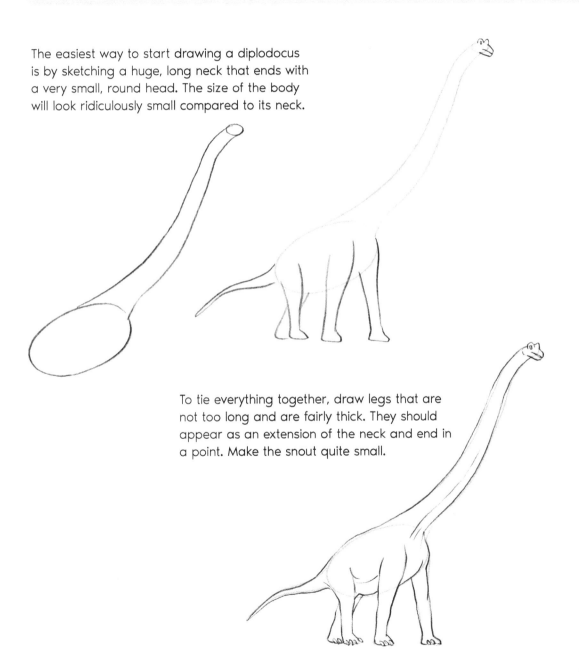

To tie everything together, draw legs that are not too long and are fairly thick. They should appear as an extension of the neck and end in a point. Make the snout quite small.

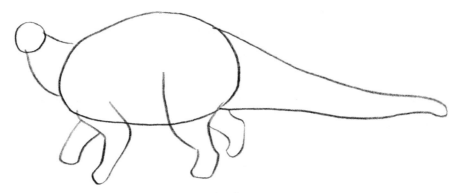

The beginning structure of the polacanthus looks similar to the diplodocus, but with a much shorter neck.

Its square snout and the spikes along its body are what make this dinosaur distinct.

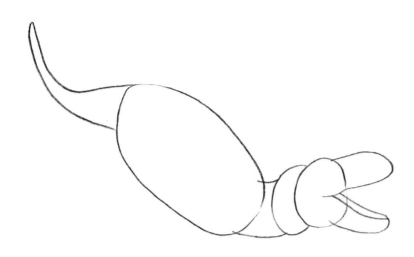

The basic forms of the tyrannosaurus are much more complex. The hind legs are huge and muscular compared to its tiny front legs, and the jaw is bulky and angular. From its claws to its teeth, everything looks scary!

FINISH YOUR DRAWING WITH AN OLD FELT-TIP MARKER

Old felt-tip markers will create a line that's not completely black and can be a little more wiggly.

Start by redrawing the outline of the dinosaur. This is the perfect opportunity to highlight the folds of skin.

Using hatching, create a few shadows and add some depth.

Gradually add new hatching on top of the first layer, changing the direction of the line to give your shadows more weight.

Finish your drawing with some dark, black lines running across the dinosaur's back to highlight more skin patterns.

T-REX PRACTICE PAGES

Try your hand at finishing the original sketch.

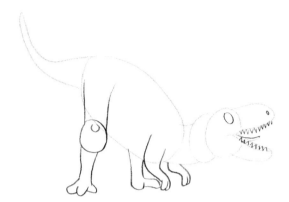

Draw your own T-Rex in the space below.

INSECTS

Start all insects with a shell by drawing a round or oval base shape over a straight line. The symmetrical details surrounding the body will help you differentiate between insects.

To draw a beetle, draw a straight line and place an oval on top that represents the back and the head.

Add lines for legs and draw the details of the head.

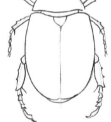

Draw the contours of the body. Thicken the legs and fill in the last few details.

In flight, the beetle takes its wings out from under its shell. Seen from above, a beetle's wings are always symmetrical.

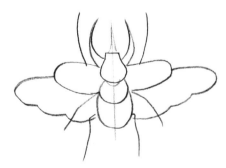

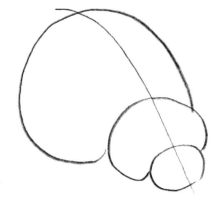

When drawing a ladybug at a three-quarter angle, its back will look like it is bulging out. So, draw the central straight line curved along the body.

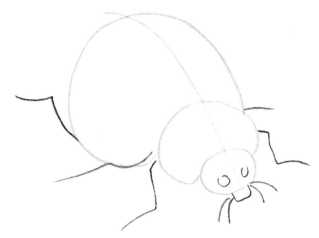

In this perspective, one of the back legs is no longer visible.

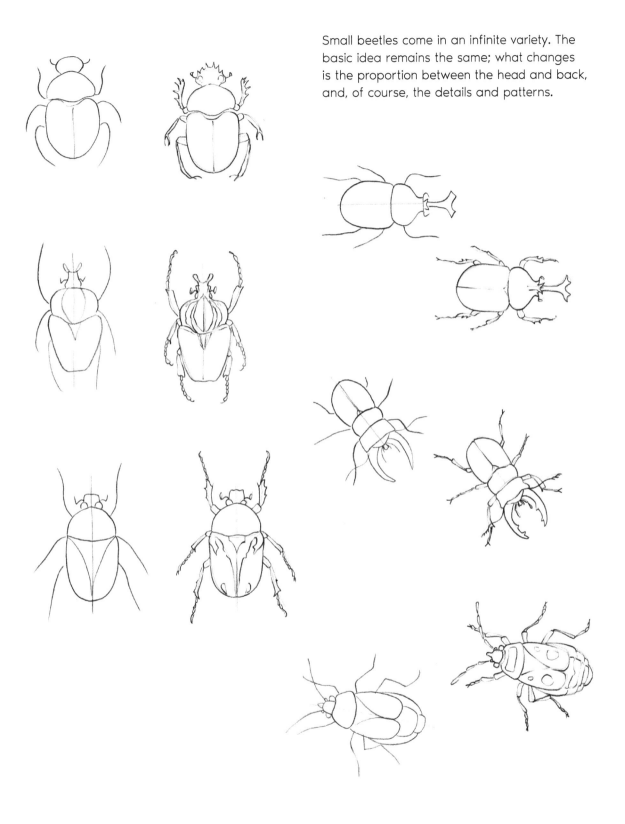

Small beetles come in an infinite variety. The basic idea remains the same; what changes is the proportion between the head and back, and, of course, the details and patterns.

FINISH YOUR DRAWING WITH A FELT-TIP MARKER AND A BALLPOINT PEN

Like the pencil, the ballpoint pen allows for lines of different intensities. You can create everything from a light gray line by pressing lightly to a thick black line by pressing harder and overlapping the lines. Felt-tips, on the other hand, will always produce very dark lines.

Start by redrawing the contours of the beetle with a ballpoint pen, and then outline some patterns.

Fill in the patterns and add areas with dark, tight hatching. You can partially overlap these shaded sections to make them more intense.

Now use the felt-tip marker to draw the outlines of the ladybug. Darken the legs and the antennae.

The ballpoint pen will help darken and add depth to several areas, with lines going in different directions. Make sure the front of the beetle is darker than the back.

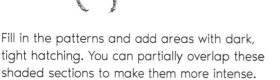

Finish by adding some spots that look like stains.

BEETLE PRACTICE PAGES

Try your hand at finishing the original sketch.

Draw your own beetle in the space below.

LADYBUG PRACTICE PAGES

Try your hand at finishing the original sketch.

Draw your own ladybug in the space below.

BLANK PRACTICE PAGES

ABOUT THE ILLUSTRATOR

LISE HERZOG was born in Alsace in 1973. She began life with a ballpoint pen in hand, her goal to fill drafts of A4 paper with her drawings. In search of precision, she observes and redraws every day, trying to figure out how to accurately represent things—and is sometimes disappointed the next day. So she starts again. This is how she began pursuing her journey at the University of Plastic Arts and then at Decorative Arts in Strasbourg. In 1999, with her diploma in her pocket, she presented her sketchbooks to publishing houses, and so began her illustrative career. That same year, she was selected to attend the Bologna Book Fair. Since then, she has illustrated many books for young people and adults, from fiction to documentaries. Lise Herzog is also the author of drawing books, including *The Easy Drawing*, *The Successful Drawing*, *Easy Color*, and *Easy Perspective and Composition* Mango editions.

DISCOVER MORE DRAWING BOOKS FROM ULYSSES PRESS

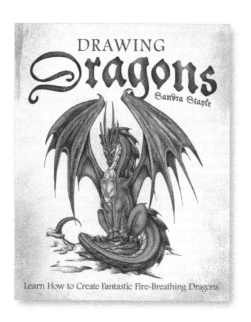

www.ulyssespress.com/drawing

Printed in the USA
CPSIA information can be obtained
at www.ICGtesting.com
CBHW062156170624
10247CB00003B/18